How To Program A Mobile Game

2nd Edition @2017
Author: Duong Tran
Cover and Text by Duong Tran

About the Author: I am also the author of my other books: Information Technology 2016, Network System Administration 2016, Cloud and Data Center, Information Technology Handbook, Network and System Administration Handbook, and How To Create An App.

About this book: As I had promised from my previous book How To Create An App, this edition add-on open source code in Swift, Java, Csharp, JavaScript and HTML. In just one time view, you will know how to program a mobile game.

Table of Contents

Mobile App Developer @Salary.com

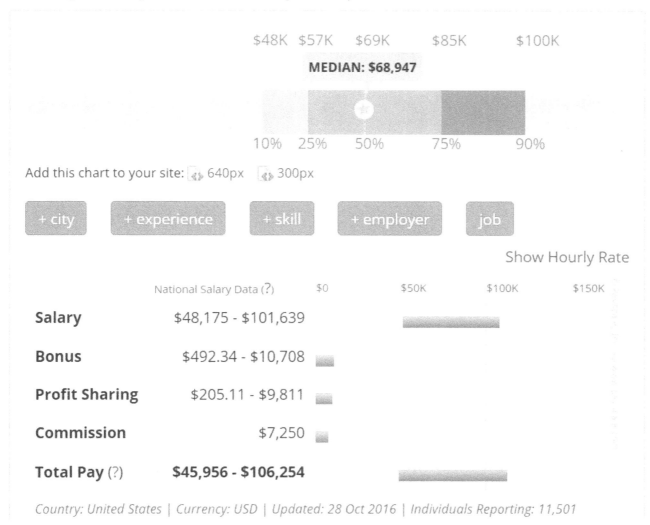

Software Developer Salary (United States)

A Software Developer earns an average salary of $68,948 per year. Most people move on to other jobs if they have more than 20 years' experience in this career.

Software developers has an average salary of $68K compared to mobile app $97K in the U.S.A. It is one of the highest paying job.

Mobile Apple Developer @VisionMobile

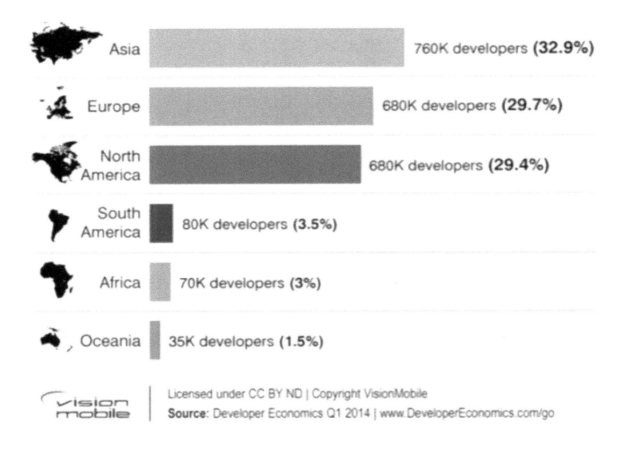

Source: VisionMobile

There are about 680K mobile developers in North America. The big three Asia, Europe and North America have the total over two millions (2,200,000) mobile developers. The industry is hiring a lot of mobile developers world wide.

Mobile App Development flow @cestarcollege.com

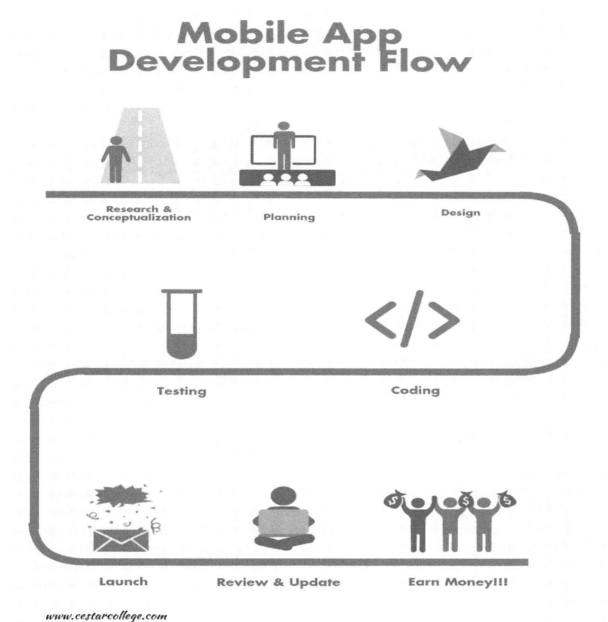

To start a mobile app, do some research first. Next, plans for the time. How to code? Which programming language? How to test using the emulator? Do some testings like user testing. Publish the app to stores and marketing.

Mobile Architecture

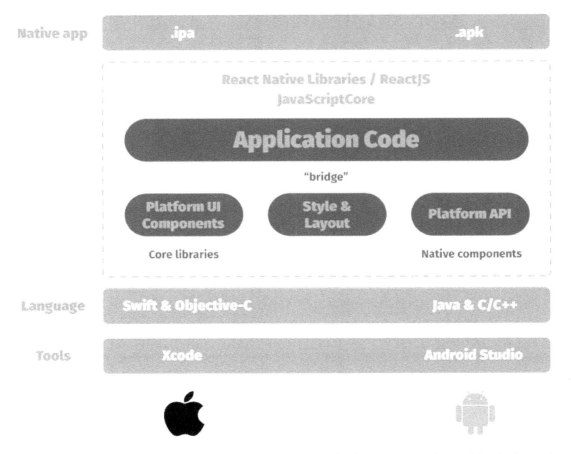

Mobile architecture components are the core libraries, platform API and graphic design. Apple Xcode is a developer tool to create iPhone app. It includes the compiler and swift programming language. The swift programming is based on Objective-C. iOS application packages are saved in the .ipa. Android Studio is another developer tool to create mobile app for Android devices with Java and C/C++ programming languages. Android application packages are saved in the zip file.apk. Microsoft introduced the Universal Windows Platform for all Windows devices based on .NET architecture. Microsoft also invested in Xamarin, a company that created a cross platform for iPhone/Android/Windows.

Mobile Architecture @Microsoft.com

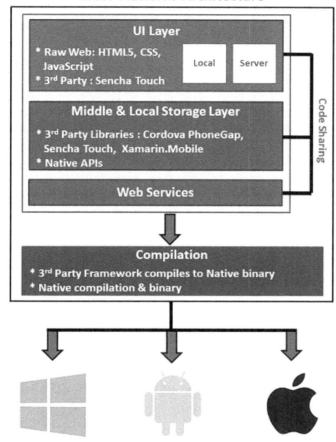

HTML5, CSS, JavaScript are web programming languages and code shared that the app is using the web service to connect to app server or game server which allows multi players and messaging. It is difference than a standard or tradition game that the user downloads to the device and plays alone.

iOS Architecture @Apple.com

Cocoa Touch supports the appearing of the screen like the AirDrop Framework which allows to share photos and documents. The TexKit Framework supports text control. UIKit Framework supports the behaviors of the objects. Address Book UI Framework allows to manage contact information. EvenKit Frameworks allows to add/edit/view calendar events. GameKit Framework supports gaming. iAD Framework allows to add advertise banner to the game. MapKit Frameworks provides map direction for the app. Message UI Framework provides messaging. Notification Framwork provides display information. PushKit Framework alerts incoming call for the app.

Media provides core graphic, audio, and video frameworks. Core Audio Frameworks are a set of frameworks to manage audio. Core Graphic Frameworks provide graphic. Core Image Frameworks provide images Core Text Frameworks provide text layout. Core Video Frameworks provide video. Other media frameworks are Game Controller Frameworks, Image I/O Frameworks, Media Accessibility Framework, Media Player Frameworks, Metal Frameworks, OpenAL Framework, OpenGL ES Framework, Photo Frameworks, Photo UI Framework, Quartz Framework, SceneKit Framework and SpriteKit Framework.

Core Services provide system services like iCloud, social media, and networking from the CloudKit Framework, Social Framework, CFNetwork Framework, Core Data Framework, Account Framework, Address Book Framework, AD Support Framework, Core Location Framework, Core Media Framework, Core Motion Framework, Core Telephony Framewor, EvenKit Framework, HealthKit Framework, HomeKit Frameowrk, JavaScript Core Framework, Mobile Core Service Framework, Multi Peer Connectivity Framework, NewstandKit Framework, PassKit Framework, QuickLook Framework, Safari Service Framework, StoreKit Framework, Core Foundation Framework, System Configuration Framework and WebKit.

Core OS provides Generic Security Services Framework, External Accessory Framework, Local Authentication Framework, Network Extension Frameworks, Security Framework and System drivers

The iOS Architecture @Apple.com

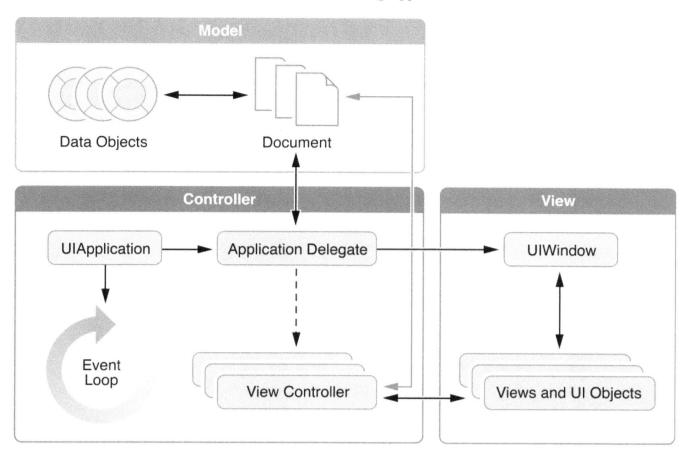

iOS apps are based on Model-View-Control architecture. In the View, the UIWindow object display the contents, windows, graphic layout, and user interface. The Controller manages how to display the View. The UIApplication object in the Controller sends the event or events to the View Controller and to the View. During the process, the app accesses the data and document from the Model. Another way to easy understand is View-Control-Model. It should be called View-Control-Data. However, the Data has its model. Anyway, the iOS apps or games are based on Model-View-Control processes.

Xcode @Apple.com

No Recent Projects

 Get started with a playground
Explore new ideas quickly and easily.

 Create a new Xcode project
Create an app for iPhone, iPad, Mac, Apple Watch or Apple TV.

 Check out an existing project
Start working on something from an SCM repository.

✅ Show this window when Xcode launches   Open another project...

Xcode 8 is the latest version built-in Swift 3 programming language. It is a compiler and interface builder. It requires Apple macOS computer. It can be downloaded at
https://developer.apple.com/xcode/

Xcode @Apple.com

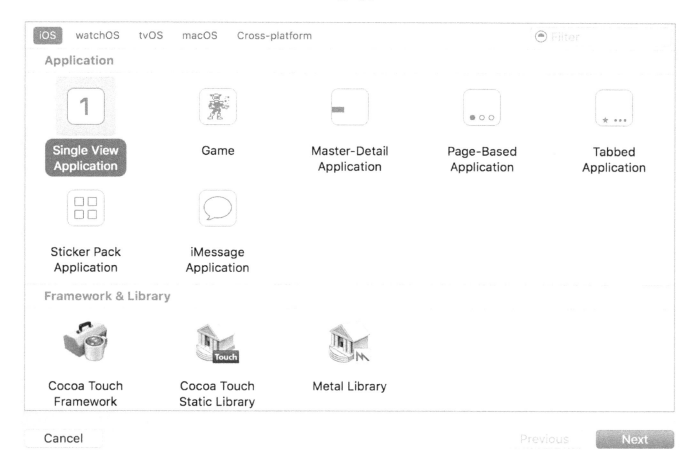

Open Xcode and choose iOS, there are some templates ready. Click on Single View Application.

Xcode @Apple.com

Choose options for your new project:

Product Name:	FoodTracker
Team:	None
Organization Name:	Apple Inc.
Organization Identifier:	com.example
Bundle Identifier:	com.example.FoodTracker
Language:	Swift
Devices:	Universal

☐ Use Core Data
☑ Include Unit Tests
☐ Include UI Tests

Cancel   Previous   Next

Name the app and the team. Choose Swift. Choose the device. Select Include Unit Tests and Include UI Tests. If Core Data is used, select Core Data. Otherwise, leave it blank.

Xcode @Apple.com

Toolbar

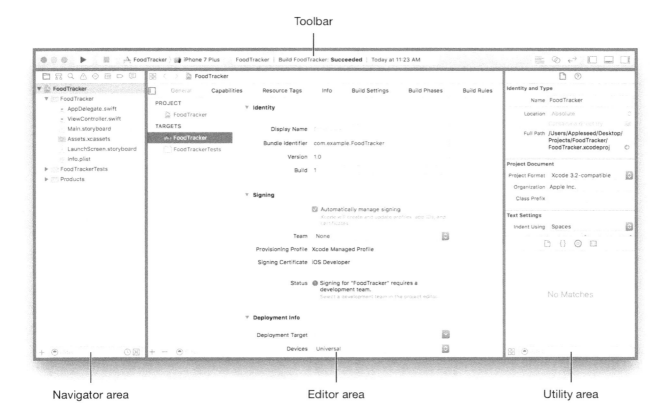

Navigator area   Editor area   Utility area

Xcode has four areas: Toolbar tabs with the emulator functions for testing devices, the Navigator area project structure, the Editor area for work space, the Utility area for settings.

Xcode @Apple.com

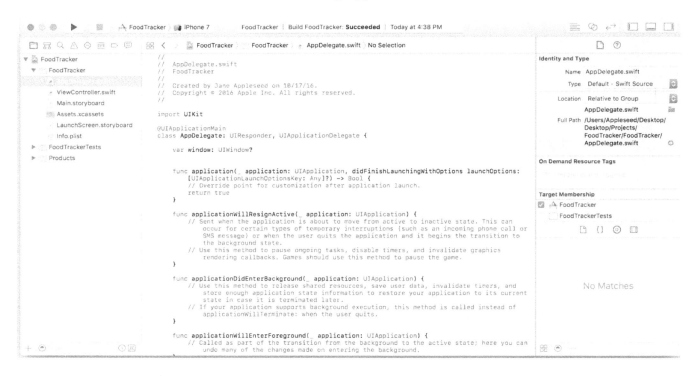

The AppDelegate.swift is the source code file. The actual binary file is the .app file. The ViewController.swift is another source code file to control the displays. The Main.storyboard is the interface builder. The Asseets.xassets contains resource files such as images. The Test folder contains test activities. If this is a framework folder, the folder contains plug-in frameworks. Another folder can be added to store the resource files. The Products folder contains the executable file .app. The native project is saved as the .ipa archive compressed file. The .ipa file structure contains the .app file, the metadata .plist file, and other app data. Objective-C programming language uses the .h and .m files for header and object implementation.

Swift language is based on C and Objective-C created by Apple. Swift includes compiler, standard library, SDK overlay and debugger. The swift file is the source file. It takes times to learn the swift programming. Many open sources and commercial frameworks are available to create mobile app quickly with no code or less coding required.

Android Architecture @Android.com

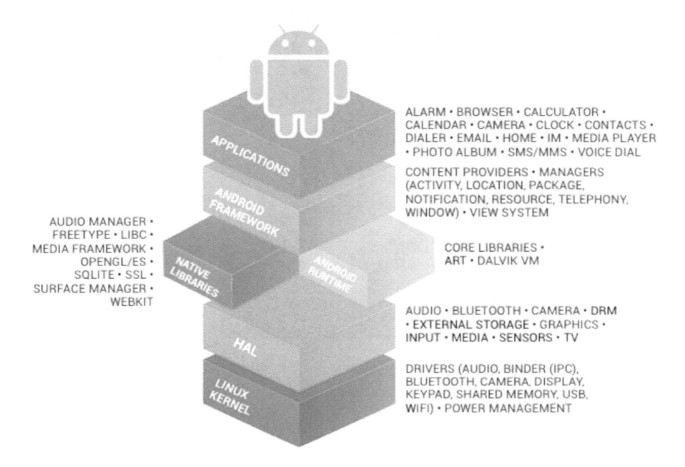

Android architecture is built on Linux Kernel. Android app cores are Android Framework, Android Runtime (Android RunTime ART and DALVIK Virtual Machine), and Native Libraries (Web engine WebKIT, 3D Graphic Libary OPENGL/ES, SQLite database, Secure Sockets Layer SSL,.etc). Android supports C/C++/Java and allows other run-times plug-in to create C# app, HTML5 and other programming languages. This means Android is an open source.

Android Architecture @Android.com

Android 7 is the latest version. The best feature of version 7 is the multi-windows.

Android Architecture @Xamarin.com

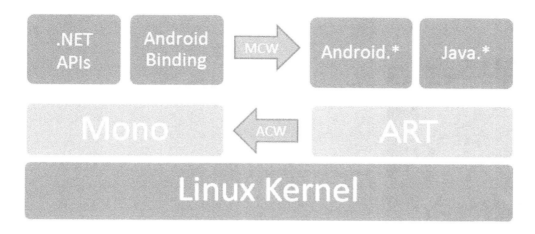

The .NET APIs use Mono runtime because it was written in C language. The Java APIs use the Android Runtime because the Android Runtime was written in Java language. Android Architecture supports both environments.

Android Studio @Android.com

Android Studio cores are Android app modules, Library modules, Google App Engine modules. Download Android Studio @ https://developer.android.com/studio/index.html

Android Studio

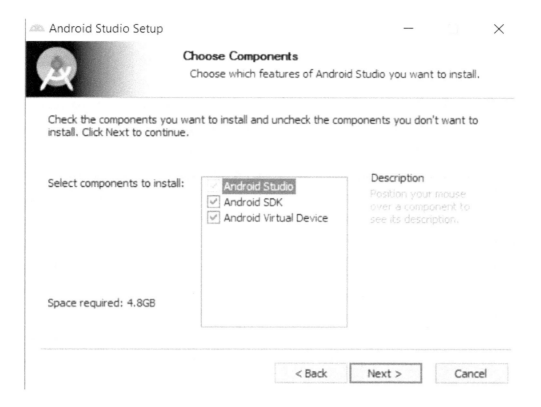

Other than the cores, the other components are the Android SDK Software Development Kit and the Android Virtual Device. Click Next and Next to complete the installation. It takes a few minutes for the installation.

Android Studio

Welcome to Android Studio   —   □   ✕

Android Studio

Version 2.2.3

☆ Start a new Android Studio project

☐ Open an existing Android Studio project

⬇ Check out project from Version Control ▾

▣ Import project (Eclipse ADT, Gradle, etc.)

▣ Import an Android code sample

⚙ Configure ▾   Get Help ▾

Android Studio 2.2.3 is the latest version

Android Studio

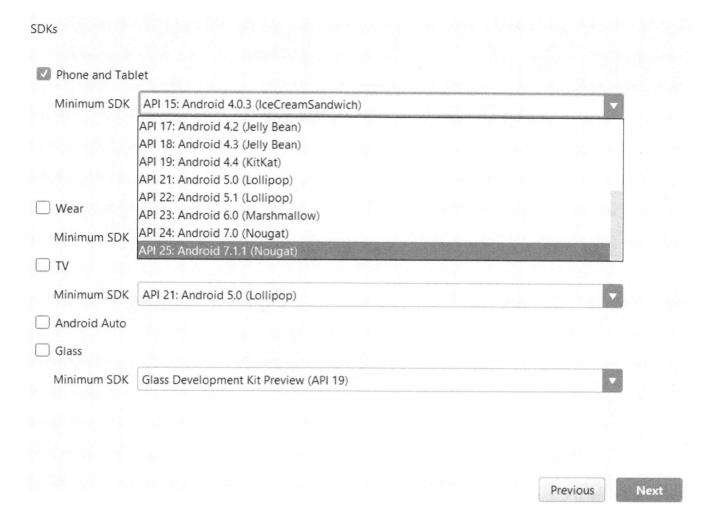

Scroll down to select Android 7.1.1

Android Studio

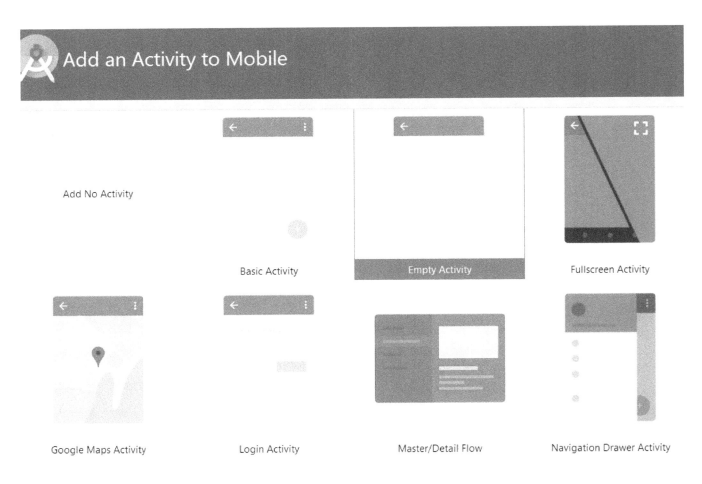

Select Empty Activity to create a blank project.

Android Studio

Configure your new project

Application name:	My Application
Company Domain:	Duong Tran
Package name:	duongtran.myapplication
	☐ Include C++ Support

Name the app and an individual/organization.

Android Studio

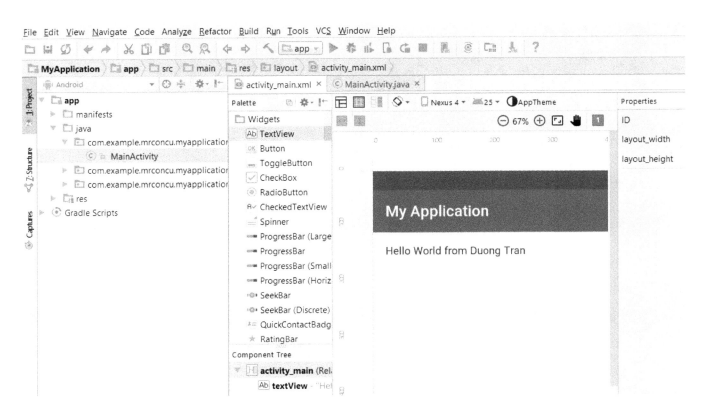

Click on the MainActivity and design the app.

Android Studio

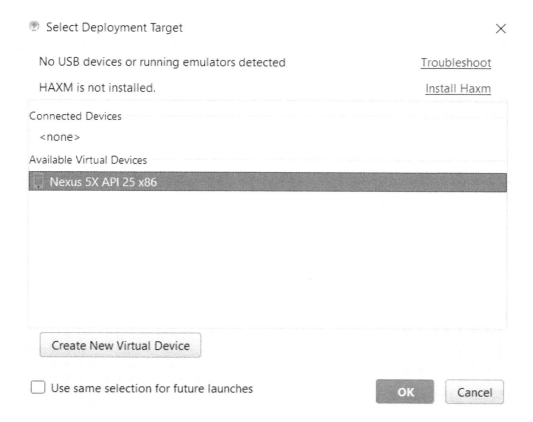

Select or create a new virtual device to run the app.

Android Studio

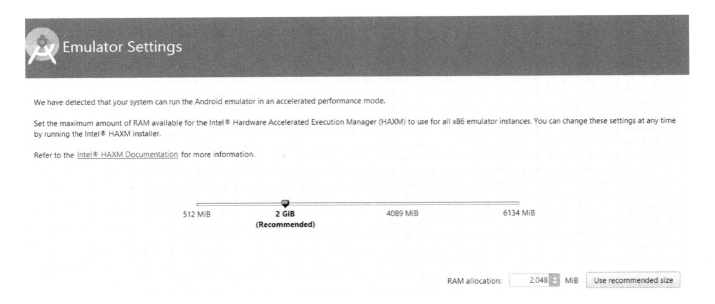

Set the virtual RAM for the simulator. It is actually used the real computer RAM.

Android Studio

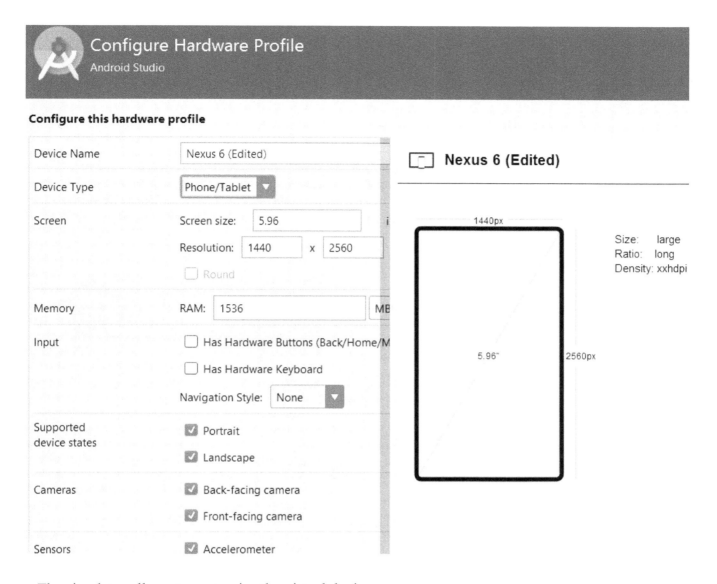

The simulator allows to customize the virtual devices.

Android Studio

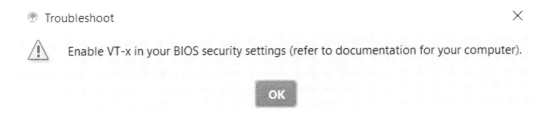

The emulator requires to restart the computer to changes the BIOS setting for the hardware chip to enable virtual technology chip. Shutdown the computer, power on, press F10 (for most computers) to enter the BIOS. In the System setting, enable Virtualization Technology, Save and Exit. Open Android Studio, another screen will pop-up to notify that Android will disable Hyper-V to use the emulator.

An update is required. It displays on the top right menu or running the emulator.

Run the app, the virtual phone will pop-up.

Universal Windows Platform @Microsoft.com

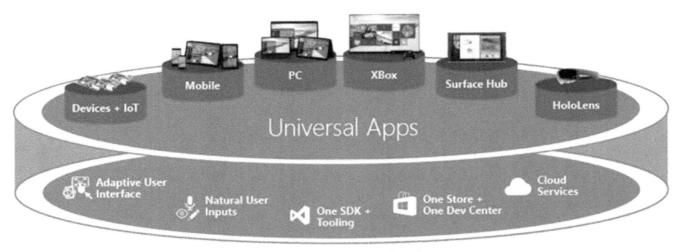

Microsoft Universal Windows Platform UWP is a run-time for Windows 10 Mobile and Windows 10 devices. It supports C++, C#, F#, VB.NET, XAML and JavaScript. Visual Studio 2015 is included UWP. Visual Studio 2015 is also included the Xamarin to develop Andriod and iOS apps.

Universal Windows Platform @Microsoft.com

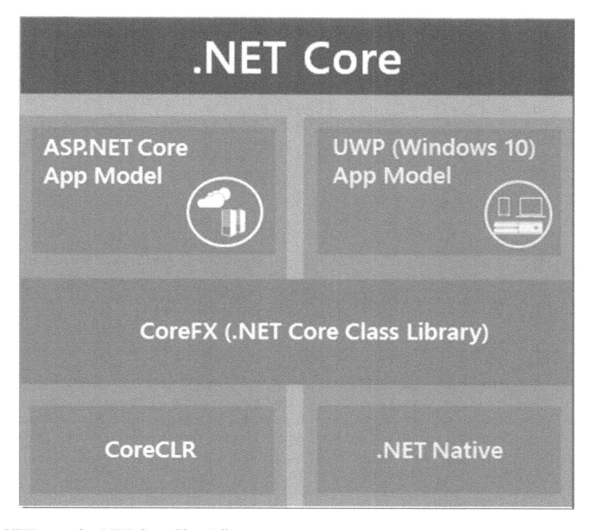

The UWP uses the .NET Core Class Library.

Universal Windows Platform @Microsoft.com

App Models	.NET Framework		.NET Core	Xamarin	
	WPF	Windows Forms	UWP	Xamarin. iOS	Xamarin. Android
	ASP.NET		ASP.NET Core*	Xamarin. Forms	Xamarin. Mac
Base Libraries	.NET Framework Class Library		CoreFx Class Library	Mono Class Library	
	Common Infrastructure				
	Compilers		Languages	Runtime components	

The original .NET Framework uses the .NET Framework Class Library. The UWP uses the CoreFx Class Library. Xamarin uses the Mono Class Library. Apps may be written in common compilers, languages, or Runtime. Microsoft adds all three together to make a big tool to use in Visual Studio. Big means many gigabytes package to download and times to install. The default installation takes about 36 GB. It also needs many more available disk space for updates, plug-in, emulator, apps. It is recommended to have a great computer with a lot of memory.

Visual Studio

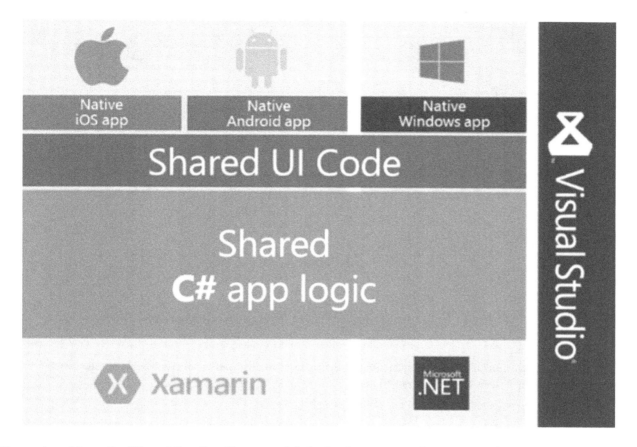

Xamarin add-on for Visual Studio allows multiple devices to use the same code C#. It includes multiple simulators.

Visual Studio @Xamarin.com

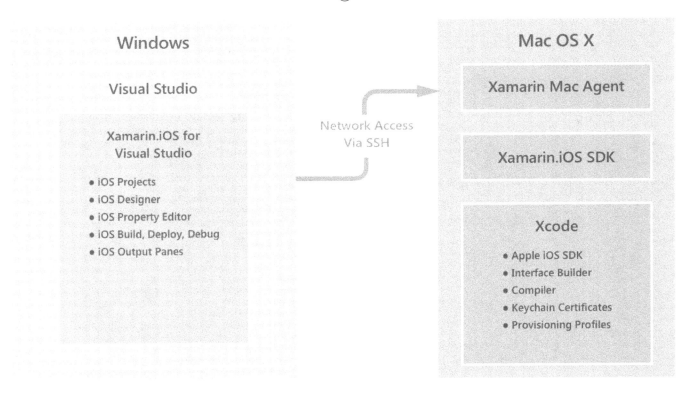

For Cross Platform, add Xamarin Mac Agent to the computer on the same network. It is nice to have an Apple computer or try to run a virtual Apple computer with VirtualBox.

Visual Studio

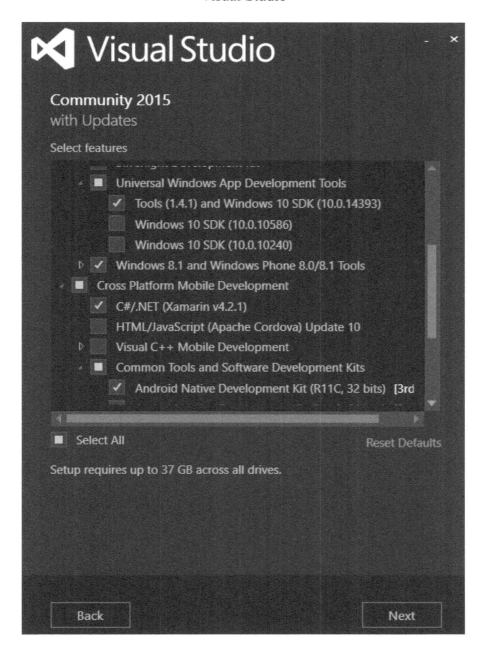

Xamarin and Visual Studio web installation is available @Xamarin.com. By default, Visual C++ Tool, Universal Window App Development Tool, Cross Platform Mobile Development C#/.NET, Android Native Development Kit(s), Android SDK and Java Development Kit are selected to install. Some others are not selected like the Visual C++ Mobile Development and HTML/JavaScript Apache Cordova.

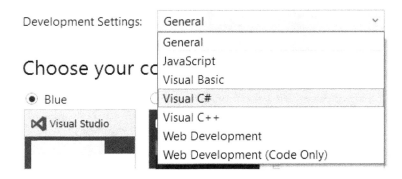

Open Visual Studio 2015, choose a programming language.

Visual Studio

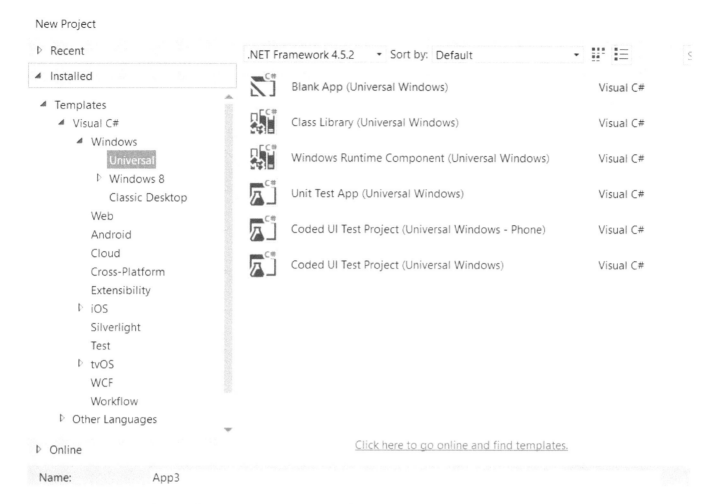

Create a New Project, select Windows, Universal, and Blank App (Universal Windows)

Visual Studio

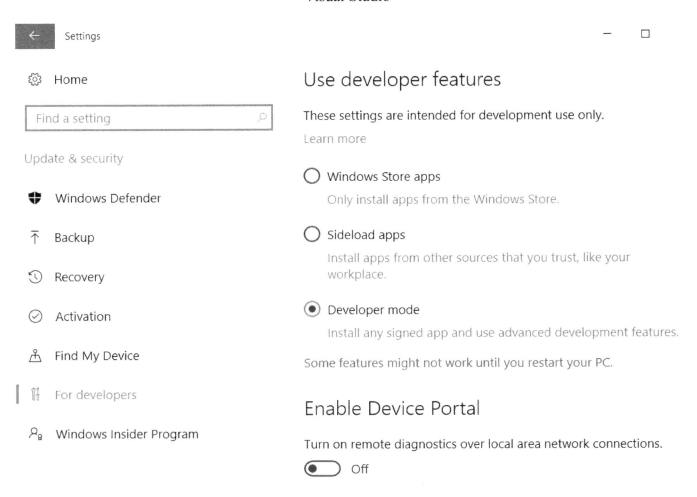

Turn on Developer mode to use the UI design in Visual Studio 2015

Visual Studio

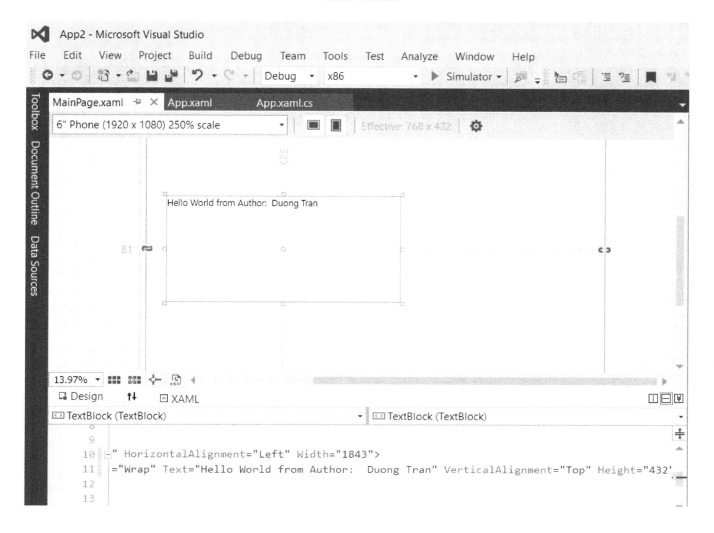

On the top left corner, Select a Windows Phone, design the interface and run the simulator.

Visual Studio

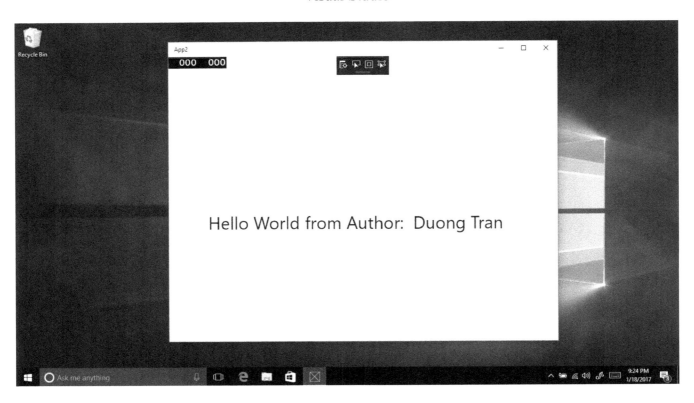

The app is running. Do not do anything wrong with the simulator other than running the app because it affects the computer.

Visual Studio

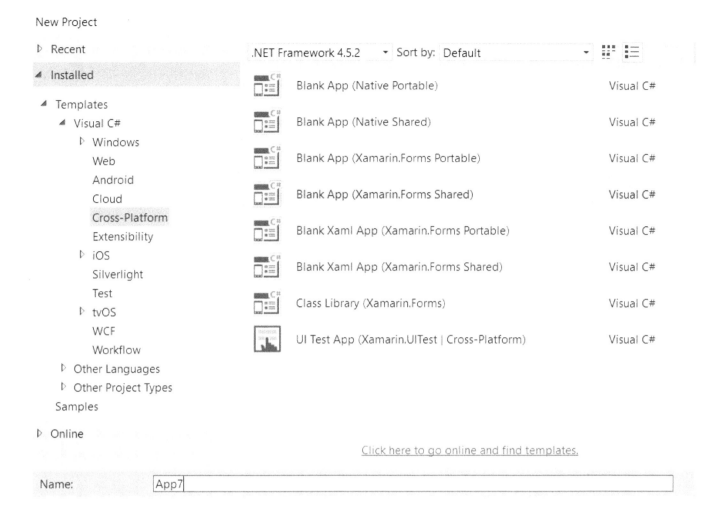

To create a shared app cross-platform for team work, open the Visual Studio and create a new project, then select Cross-Platform and select a shared template.

Visual Studio

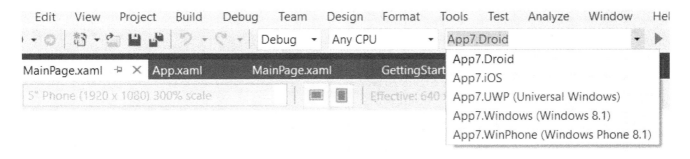

Cross Platform Shared Project has multiple simulators. For iOS, it requires MAC OS computer. Alternately, The developer can try VirtualBox to run MAC OS and Xcode, but it is outside the scope of this book.

Visual Studio

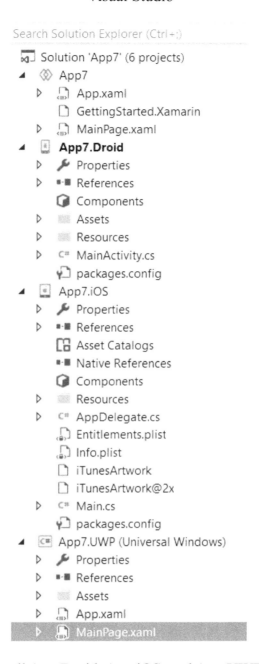

Solution Explorer Bar displays all App.Droid, App.iOS, and App.UWP shared project files.

Flappy Bird using Swift

```swift
let groundTexture = SKTexture(imageNamed: "land")
    groundTexture.filteringMode = .nearest // shorter form for SKTextureFilteringMode.Nearest

    let moveGroundSprite = SKAction.moveBy(x: -groundTexture.size().width * 2.0, y: 0,
duration: TimeInterval(0.02 * groundTexture.size().width * 2.0))
    let resetGroundSprite = SKAction.moveBy(x: groundTexture.size().width * 2.0, y: 0, duration:
0.0)
    let moveGroundSpritesForever =
SKAction.repeatForever(SKAction.sequence([moveGroundSprite,resetGroundSprite]))

    for i in 0 ..< 2 + Int(self.frame.size.width / ( groundTexture.size().width * 2 )) {
        let i = CGFloat(i)
        let sprite = SKSpriteNode(texture: groundTexture)
        sprite.setScale(2.0)
        sprite.position = CGPoint(x: i * sprite.size.width, y: sprite.size.height / 2.0)
        sprite.run(moveGroundSpritesForever)
        moving.addChild(sprite)
}
```

Author: This is the ground texture using SpriteKit through out the Swift code to load the asset and set the ground grass texture and moving it.

```swift
 // create the ground
    let ground = SKNode()
    ground.position = CGPoint(x: 0, y: groundTexture.size().height)
    ground.physicsBody = SKPhysicsBody(rectangleOf: CGSize(width: self.frame.size.width,
height: groundTexture.size().height * 2.0))
    ground.physicsBody?.isDynamic = false
    ground.physicsBody?.categoryBitMask = worldCategory
self.addChild(ground)
```

Author: Set the ground position, use the rectangle for texture, add the ground

Flappy Bird using Swift

```swift
let skyTexture = SKTexture(imageNamed: "sky")
    skyTexture.filteringMode = .nearest

    let moveSkySprite = SKAction.moveBy(x: -skyTexture.size().width * 2.0, y: 0, duration:
TimeInterval(0.1 * skyTexture.size().width * 2.0))
    let resetSkySprite = SKAction.moveBy(x: skyTexture.size().width * 2.0, y: 0, duration: 0.0)
    let moveSkySpritesForever =
SKAction.repeatForever(SKAction.sequence([moveSkySprite,resetSkySprite]))

    for i in 0 ..< 2 + Int(self.frame.size.width / ( skyTexture.size().width * 2 )) {
        let i = CGFloat(i)
        let sprite = SKSpriteNode(texture: skyTexture)
        sprite.setScale(2.0)
        sprite.zPosition = -20
        sprite.position = CGPoint(x: i * sprite.size.width, y: sprite.size.height / 2.0 +
groundTexture.size().height * 2.0)
        sprite.run(moveSkySpritesForever)
        moving.addChild(sprite)
}
```

Author: This code is similiar to the above to set the sky texture and moving it.

Flappy Bird using Swift

```
// create the pipes textures
    pipeTextureUp = SKTexture(imageNamed: "PipeUp")
    pipeTextureUp.filteringMode = .nearest
    pipeTextureDown = SKTexture(imageNamed: "PipeDown")
    pipeTextureDown.filteringMode = .nearest

    // create the pipes movement actions
    let distanceToMove = CGFloat(self.frame.size.width + 2.0 * pipeTextureUp.size().width)
    let movePipes = SKAction.moveBy(x: -distanceToMove, y:0.0, duration:TimeInterval(0.01 *
distanceToMove))
    let removePipes = SKAction.removeFromParent()
    movePipesAndRemove = SKAction.sequence([movePipes, removePipes])

    // spawn the pipes
    let spawn = SKAction.run(spawnPipes)
    let delay = SKAction.wait(forDuration: TimeInterval(2.0))
    let spawnThenDelay = SKAction.sequence([spawn, delay])
    let spawnThenDelayForever = SKAction.repeatForever(spawnThenDelay)
self.run(spawnThenDelayForever)
```

Author: First code is the pipe texture, using the pipe texture to create the pipe, and moving it with SKAction.moveBy, removed by SKAction.removeFromParent(), repeated the action by SKAAction.sequence.

Flappy Bird using Swift

```
// setup our bird
    let birdTexture1 = SKTexture(imageNamed: "bird-01")
    birdTexture1.filteringMode = .nearest
    let birdTexture2 = SKTexture(imageNamed: "bird-02")
    birdTexture2.filteringMode = .nearest

    let anim = SKAction.animate(with: [birdTexture1, birdTexture2], timePerFrame: 0.2)
    let flap = SKAction.repeatForever(anim)

    bird = SKSpriteNode(texture: birdTexture1)
    bird.setScale(2.0)
    bird.position = CGPoint(x: self.frame.size.width * 0.35, y:self.frame.size.height * 0.6)
    bird.run(flap)


    bird.physicsBody = SKPhysicsBody(circleOfRadius: bird.size.height / 2.0)
    bird.physicsBody?.isDynamic = true
    bird.physicsBody?.allowsRotation = false

    bird.physicsBody?.categoryBitMask = birdCategory
    bird.physicsBody?.collisionBitMask = worldCategory | pipeCategory
    bird.physicsBody?.contactTestBitMask = worldCategory | pipeCategory

self.addChild(bird)
```

Author: Create the texture for the bird, make it animated, set the size and position. The bird is flying. Also, check for the collision with the pipe bird.physicsBody?.collisionBitMask = worldCategory | pipeCategory

Flappy Bird using Java

```java
public class FBGame extends Game {
    /**
     * Creates the game
     */
    @Override
    public void create() {
            AssetLoader.load(); // Load all assets (game data)
            setScreen(new GameScreen()); // Create the game screen to display the game
    }

    /**
     * Dispose the game
     */
    @Override
    public void dispose() {
            super.dispose(); // Kill game process
            AssetLoader.dispose(); // Dispose all assets
    }

}
```

Author: Create a class and a function to load the assets AssetLoader() and new screen GameScreen() from the function of other classes.

Flappy Bird using Java

```java
public class AssetLoader {
        public static Texture texture; // Texture from which the game graphics will be created
        public static TextureRegion bg, grass, bird, birdDown, birdUp, barUp, barDown, bar, logo,
fbLogo, startButton, ready, gameOver, scoreBoard; // Texture regions created from the texture file
        public static Animation animation; // Animation of the bird when it flies
        public static Sound dead, flap, coin, fall; // Sound files
        public static BitmapFont font, shadow; // Fonts for displaying scores and messages
        public static Preferences prefs; // Used for saving high score. It is a map between a string
and an int in this case.

        public static void load() {
                texture = new Texture(Gdx.files.internal("data/texture.png"));
                texture.setFilter(TextureFilter.Nearest, TextureFilter.Nearest);
                bg = new TextureRegion(texture, 0, 0, 225, 400); // Background
                bg.flip(false, true);

                startButton = new TextureRegion(texture, 562, 196, 62, 22);
                startButton.flip(false, true);
                ready = new TextureRegion(texture, 462, 94, 133, 30);
                ready.flip(false, true);
                gameOver = new TextureRegion(texture, 618, 93, 147, 27);
                gameOver.flip(false, true);
                fbLogo = new TextureRegion(texture, 550, 145, 132, 25);
                fbLogo.flip(false, true);

                grass = new TextureRegion(texture, 455, 1, 265, 87);
                grass.flip(false, true);

                birdDown = new TextureRegion(texture, 180, 555, 25, 18);
                birdDown.flip(false, true);

                bird = new TextureRegion(texture, 180, 514, 25, 18);
                bird.flip(false, true);

                birdUp = new TextureRegion(texture, 180, 595, 25, 18);
                birdUp.flip(false, true);

                TextureRegion[] birds = {birdDown, bird, birdUp};
                animation = new Animation(0.06f, birds); // Animation will play using the 3 texture
regions in the birds array, every 0.06s
                animation.setPlayMode(Animation.PlayMode.LOOP_PINGPONG); // Play the
animation in the specified way

                barUp = new TextureRegion(texture, 1, 506, 40, 18);
                barDown = new TextureRegion(barUp);
                barDown.flip(false, true);
```

```
        bar = new TextureRegion(texture, 1, 535, 40, 3);
        bar.flip(false, true);

        dead = Gdx.audio.newSound(Gdx.files.internal("data/dead.wav"));
        flap = Gdx.audio.newSound(Gdx.files.internal("data/flap.wav"));
        coin = Gdx.audio.newSound(Gdx.files.internal("data/coin.wav"));
        fall = Gdx.audio.newSound(Gdx.files.internal("data/fall.wav"));

        font = new BitmapFont(Gdx.files.internal("data/text.fnt"));
        font.getData().setScale(0.25f, -0.25f);
        shadow = new BitmapFont(Gdx.files.internal("data/shadow.fnt"));
        shadow.getData().setScale(0.25f, -0.25f);

        prefs = Gdx.app.getPreferences("FlappyBird"); // App preferences used to store the
high-score
        if (!prefs.contains("highScore")) { // Initialize the high-score to 0 if not already set
                prefs.putInteger("highScore", 0);
        }
    }
}
```

Author: The class AssetLoad has the load() to import the images.

Flappy Bird using Java

```java
public GameScreen() {
        float screenWidth = Gdx.graphics.getWidth();
        float screenHeight = Gdx.graphics.getHeight();
        float gameWidth = 136;
        float gameHeight = screenHeight / (screenWidth / gameWidth);
        int yMidPoint = (int) (gameHeight / 2);

        world = new GameWorld(yMidPoint);
        Gdx.input.setInputProcessor(new InputHandler(world, screenWidth / gameWidth,
screenHeight /gameHeight));
        renderer = new GameRenderer(world, (int) gameHeight, yMidPoint);
}
```

In the GameScreen class, customize the screen size by width and height. Find the mid point to set
the bird position. It needs a texture too. Functions are called in order GameWorld(),
InputHandler(), GameRenderer().

```java
@Override
    public void render(float delta) {
        runTime += delta;
        world.update(delta);
        renderer.render(delta, runTime);
}
```

Author: This function calls the GameWorld.update() and GameRenderer.render() to override.

Flappy Bird using Java

```
public GameWorld(int yMidPoint) {
            current = GameState.MENU; // start on the menu screen
            bird = new Bird(BIRD_X_POSITION, yMidPoint - 5, BIRD_WIDTH,
BIRD_HEIGHT);
            scrollHandler = new ScrollHandler(yMidPoint + 66, this);
            ground = new Rectangle(0, yMidPoint + 66, 137, 11);
            this.yMidPoint = yMidPoint;
}
```

In the GameWorld Class, Start th menu, create the bird from the Bird(), call ScrollHandler for scrolling, and create a new texture.

```
public void update (float delta) {
            runTime += delta;
            switch (current) {
                  case READY:
                        updateReady(delta);
                        break;
                  case MENU:
                        updateReady(delta);
                        break;
                  case RUNNING:
                        updateRunning(delta);
                        break;
                  default:
                        break;
            }

}
```

Author: Game status menu to call updateReady and updateRunning().

Flappy Bird using Java

```java
public void updateRunning(float delta) {
        if (delta > 0.15f) {
                delta = 0.15f; // delta cap for when the game takes too long to update,
collision detection is not affected
        }

        // call update on the bird and the scroll handler
        bird.update(delta);
        scrollHandler.update(delta);

        // when collision is detected
        if (scrollHandler.collides(bird) && bird.isAlive()) {
                scrollHandler.stop();
                bird.die();
                AssetLoader.dead.play();
                AssetLoader.fall.play(0.5f);
        }

        // when the bird hits the ground
        if (Intersector.overlaps(bird.getCircle(), ground)) {
                if (bird.isAlive()) {
                        AssetLoader.dead.play();
                        bird.die();
                }
                scrollHandler.stop();
                bird.decelerate();
                current = GameState.GAMEOVER;
                // set high-score
                if (score > AssetLoader.getHighScore()) {
                        AssetLoader.setHighScore(score);
                        current = GameState.HIGHSCORE;
                }
        }
}
```

Author: This function will be used by GameRenderer to check object activities. It updates the bird by calling bird.update(), scrolling from scrollHandler.update, and detect collision by calling scrollHandler.collides(), bird.isAlive(), and Intersector.overlaps(). If the bird is die, call scrollHandler.stop(), bird.die(), AssetLoader.dead.play(), AssetLoad.fall.play(), and getHighScore().

Flappy Bird using Java

```java
public Bird(float x, float y, int width, int height) {
            this.width = width;
            this.height = height;
            originalY = y;
            position = new Vector2(x, y);
            velocity = new Vector2(0, 0);
            acceleration = new Vector2(0, 460);
            circle = new Circle(); // Used for collision detection
            isAlive = true;
    }
```

Author: In the Bird class, set width, eight, position, velocity, acceration.

```java
public void update(float delta) {
            velocity.add(acceleration.cpy().scl(delta));
            if (velocity.y > 200) { // Set max velocity
                velocity.y = 200;
            }
            if (velocity.y < 0) { // When the bird is flying up
                rotation -= 600 * delta; // Rotate bird
                if (rotation < -20) { // Do not rotate more than 20 degrees
                    rotation = -20;
                }
            }
            if (isFalling() || !isAlive) { // When the bird is falling
                rotation += 480 * delta;
                if (rotation > 90) {
                    rotation = 90;
                }
            }

            if (position.y < -13) { // Ceiling check (cap how far up the bird can go up)
                position.y = -13;
                velocity.y = 0;
            }
            position.add(velocity.cpy().scl(delta)); // Move the bird forward constantly
            circle.set(position.x + 9, position.y + 6, 6.5f); // Set the circle to the new position of
the bird
    }
```

Author: Update the bird position and life status, the bird will be rotate if it is dead.

Flappy Bird using Java

```
public ScrollHandler(float yPos, GameWorld world) {
            frontGrass = new Grass(0, yPos, 143, 87, SCROLL_SPEED);
            backGrass = new Grass(frontGrass.getTailX(), yPos, 143, 87, SCROLL_SPEED);
            firstPipe = new Pipe(210, 0, 22, 60, SCROLL_SPEED, yPos);
            secondPipe = new Pipe(firstPipe.getTailX() + PIPE_GAP, 0, 22, 70,
SCROLL_SPEED, yPos);
            thirdPipe = new Pipe(secondPipe.getTailX() + PIPE_GAP, 0, 22, 60,
SCROLL_SPEED, yPos);
            this.world = world;
}
```

Author: Set the scrolling speed for grass, pipe, and the bird.

```
public void update(float delta) {
            frontGrass.update(delta);
            backGrass.update(delta);
            firstPipe.update(delta);
            secondPipe.update(delta);
            thirdPipe.update(delta);

            // scroll pipes
            if (firstPipe.isScrolledLeft()) {
                    firstPipe.reset(thirdPipe.getTailX() + PIPE_GAP);
            }
            else if (secondPipe.isScrolledLeft()) {
                    secondPipe.reset(firstPipe.getTailX() + PIPE_GAP);
            }
            else if (thirdPipe.isScrolledLeft()) {
                    thirdPipe.reset(secondPipe.getTailX() + PIPE_GAP);
            }

            // scroll grass
            if (frontGrass.isScrolledLeft()) {
                    frontGrass.reset(backGrass.getTailX());
            }
            else if (backGrass.isScrolledLeft()) {
                    backGrass.reset(frontGrass.getTailX());
            }
}
```

Author: The update() for ScrollHandler class by moving the pipe to the left and reset.

Flappy Bird using Java

```java
public boolean collides(Bird bird) {
        if (!firstPipe.isScored() && firstPipe.getX() + firstPipe.getWidth() / 2 < (bird.getX()
+ bird.getWidth())) {
                world.addScore(1);
                firstPipe.setScored(true);
                AssetLoader.coin.play(0.10f);
        }
        else if (!secondPipe.isScored() && secondPipe.getX() + secondPipe.getWidth() / 2 <
(bird.getX() + bird.getWidth())) {
                world.addScore(1);
                secondPipe.setScored(true);
                AssetLoader.coin.play(0.10f);
        }
        else if (!thirdPipe.isScored() && thirdPipe.getX() + thirdPipe.getWidth() / 2 <
(bird.getX() + bird.getWidth())) {
                world.addScore(1);
                thirdPipe.setScored(true);
                AssetLoader.coin.play(0.10f);
        }
        return (firstPipe.collides(bird) || secondPipe.collides(bird) || thirdPipe.collides(bird));
    }
```

Author: The collides in this ScrollHandler class is called by the GameWorld class to check the collision by checking the intersection of the pipe and the bird.

Flappy Bird using Java

```java
public GameRenderer(GameWorld world, int gameHeight, int yMidPoint) {
        this.world = world;
        this.gameHeight = gameHeight;
        this.yMidPoint = yMidPoint;
        startButton = ((InputHandler) Gdx.input.getInputProcessor()).getStartButton();

        cam = new OrthographicCamera();
        cam.setToOrtho(true, 136, gameHeight);

        batcher = new SpriteBatch();
        batcher.setProjectionMatrix(cam.combined); // Attach batcher to camera

        shapeRenderer = new ShapeRenderer();
        shapeRenderer.setProjectionMatrix(cam.combined);

        initGameObjects();
        initAssets();
}
```

Author: In the GameRenderer, create all the textures for all objects like drawBrid(), drawPipes(), drawGrass(), and others. This class imports other frameworks in the headers to create 2d graphic.

```java
import com.badlogic.gdx.Gdx;
import com.badlogic.gdx.graphics.GL20;
import com.badlogic.gdx.graphics.OrthographicCamera;
import com.badlogic.gdx.graphics.g2d.Animation;
import com.badlogic.gdx.graphics.g2d.SpriteBatch;
import com.badlogic.gdx.graphics.g2d.TextureRegion;
import com.badlogic.gdx.graphics.glutils.ShapeRenderer;
```

Flappy Bird using Java

```java
public void render(float delta, float runTime) {
        // Fill Screen with black to prevent flickering
        Gdx.gl.glClearColor(0, 0, 0, 1);
        Gdx.gl.glClear(GL20.GL_COLOR_BUFFER_BIT);

        batcher.begin();
        // disable transparency to improve performance
        batcher.disableBlending();
        batcher.draw(AssetLoader.bg, 0, 0, 136, gameHeight);

        drawGrass();
        drawPipes();
        drawPipeEnds();

        batcher.enableBlending(); // bird needs transparency
        // Draw bird at its coordinates, retrieve animation from AssetLoader, pass runTime to
get current frame
        if (world.isRunning() || world.isHighScore()) {
                drawBird(runTime);
                drawScore();
        }

        else if (world.isReady()) {
                drawBird(runTime);
                drawScore();
                drawReady();
        }

        else if (world.isGameOver()) {
                drawBird(runTime);
                drawGameOver();
        }

        else if (world.isMenu()) {
                drawBirdCentered(runTime);
                drawMenuUI();
        }


        if (world.isReady()) {
                AssetLoader.shadow.draw(batcher, "Touch Me", 26, 75);
                AssetLoader.font.draw(batcher, "Touch Me", 27, 75);
        }
        else {
                if (world.isGameOver() || world.isHighScore()) {
                        if (world.isGameOver()) {
```

```
                              AssetLoader.shadow.draw(batcher, "High Score:", 23, 106);
                              AssetLoader.font.draw(batcher, "High Score:", 22, 105);
                              String highScore = AssetLoader.getHighScore() + "";
                              AssetLoader.shadow.draw(batcher, highScore, 68 - (3 *
highScore.length()), 128);
                              AssetLoader.font.draw(batcher, highScore, 68 - (3 *
highScore.length() - 1), 127);

                              AssetLoader.shadow.draw(batcher, "Tap to Retry", 10, 76);
                              AssetLoader.font.draw(batcher, "Tap to Retry", 11, 75);
                          }
                     else {
          AssetLoader.shadow.draw(batcher, "High Score!", 23, 56);
          AssetLoader.font.draw(batcher, "High Score!", 22, 55);
                     }
                 }
            }
          batcher.end();
    }
}
```

Author: The render function in this GameRenderer class creates the texture and draw all objects.

Flappy Bird using Java

```
/**
     * Initializes game objects
     */
private void initGameObjects() {
    bird = world.getBird();
    scrollHandler = world.getScrollHandler();
    frontGrass = scrollHandler.getFrontGrass();
    backGrass = scrollHandler.getBackGrass();
    firstPipe = scrollHandler.getFirstPipe();
    secondPipe = scrollHandler.getSecondPipe();
    thirdPipe = scrollHandler.getThirdPipe();
}

    /**
     * Loads and initializes assets from the AssetLoader class
     */
private void initAssets() {
    bg = AssetLoader.bg;
    grass = AssetLoader.grass;
    animation = AssetLoader.animation;
    birdMid = AssetLoader.bird;
    barUp = AssetLoader.barUp;
    barDown = AssetLoader.barDown;
    bar = AssetLoader.bar;
    ready = AssetLoader.ready;
    fbLogo = AssetLoader.fbLogo;
    gameOver = AssetLoader.gameOver;
}
```

Author: Get the objects and load the images.

Flappy Bird using Java

```
private void drawBirdCentered(float runTime) {
    batcher.draw(animation.getKeyFrame(runTime),
                    59,
                    bird.getY() - 15,
            bird.getWidth() / 2.0f, bird.getHeight() / 2.0f,
            bird.getWidth(), bird.getHeight(), 1, 1, bird.getRotation());
}

    /**
     * Draws the bird while the game is running
     * @param runTime
     *                      runtime of the game
     */


public void drawBird(float runTime) {
        if (bird.noFlap()) {
                batcher.draw(birdMid, bird.getX(), bird.getY(), bird.getWidth() / 2.0f,
bird.getHeight() / 2.0f, bird.getWidth(), bird.getHeight(), 1, 1, bird.getRotation());
        }
        else {
                batcher.draw(AssetLoader.animation.getKeyFrame(runTime), bird.getX(),
bird.getY(), bird.getWidth() / 2.0f,
                                        bird.getHeight() / 2.0f, bird.getWidth(),
bird.getHeight(), 1, 1, bird.getRotation());
        }
}
```

Author: The function uses SpriteBatch to draw the bird.

Flappy Bird using Java

```
/**
        * Draws the grass
        */
private void drawGrass() {
        batcher.draw(grass, frontGrass.getX(), frontGrass.getY(), frontGrass.getWidth() + 1,
frontGrass.getHeight());
        batcher.draw(grass, backGrass.getX(), backGrass.getY(), backGrass.getWidth() + 1,
backGrass.getHeight());
    }
```

Author: Both front and background grass add one per frame.

Flappy Bird using Java

```
    /**
     * Draws the pipe ends
     */
private void drawPipeEnds() {
        batcher.draw(barUp, firstPipe.getX() - 1, firstPipe.getY() +  firstPipe.getHeight() - 14, 24,
14);
        batcher.draw(barDown, firstPipe.getX() - 1, firstPipe.getY() +  firstPipe.getHeight() + 45,
24, 14);

        batcher.draw(barUp, secondPipe.getX() - 1, secondPipe.getY() +  secondPipe.getHeight() -
14, 24, 14);
        batcher.draw(barDown, secondPipe.getX() - 1, secondPipe.getY() +  secondPipe.getHeight()
+ 45, 24, 14);

        batcher.draw(barUp, thirdPipe.getX() - 1, thirdPipe.getY() +  thirdPipe.getHeight() - 14, 24,
14);
        batcher.draw(barDown, thirdPipe.getX() - 1, thirdPipe.getY() +  thirdPipe.getHeight() + 45,
24, 14);
    }
```

Author: Each pipe ends by -1

```
    /**
     * Draws the pipes
     */
private void drawPipes() {
        batcher.draw(bar, firstPipe.getX(), firstPipe.getY(), firstPipe.getWidth(),
firstPipe.getHeight());
        batcher.draw(bar, firstPipe.getX(), firstPipe.getY() + firstPipe.getHeight() + 45,
firstPipe.getWidth(), yMidPoint + 66 - (firstPipe.getHeight() + 45));

        batcher.draw(bar, secondPipe.getX(), secondPipe.getY(), secondPipe.getWidth(),
secondPipe.getHeight());
        batcher.draw(bar, secondPipe.getX(), secondPipe.getY() + secondPipe.getHeight() + 45,
secondPipe.getWidth(), yMidPoint + 66 - (secondPipe.getHeight() + 45));

        batcher.draw(bar, thirdPipe.getX(), thirdPipe.getY(), thirdPipe.getWidth(),
thirdPipe.getHeight());
        batcher.draw(bar, thirdPipe.getX(), thirdPipe.getY() + thirdPipe.getHeight() + 45,
thirdPipe.getWidth(), yMidPoint + 66 - (thirdPipe.getHeight() + 45));
}
```

Author: A set of three textures for three pipes.

Flappy Bird using Java

```
public InputHandler(GameWorld world, float scaleX, float scaleY) {
        this.world = world;
        bird = world.getBird();
        int yMidPoint = world.getYMidPoint();
        this.scaleX = scaleX;
        this.scaleY = scaleY;
        play = new Button(82 - (AssetLoader.startButton.getRegionWidth() / 2), yMidPoint
+ 25, 29, 16, AssetLoader.startButton);
}
```

Author When the user press the button, this function will load the asset. startButton is a new texture region. This is used GameScreen class and GameRenderer class.

```
public Button(float x, float y, float width, float height, TextureRegion startButton) {
        this.x = x;
        this.y = y;
        this.width = width;
        this.height = height;
        this.startButton = startButton;
        bounds = new Rectangle(x, y, width, height);
}
```

Author: In the Button class, the Button funtion create a new rectangle texture.

Flappy Bird using Java

```java
public class Grass extends Scrollable {

    public Grass(float x, float y, int width, int height, float scrollSpeed) {
        super(x, y, width, height, scrollSpeed);
    }
}
```

Author: Create a Grass class and use the Scrollable class, return the grass position, size and scroll speed.

Flappy Bird using Java

```java
public Pipe(float x, float y, int width, int height, float scrollSpeed, float yGround) {
        super(x, y, width, height, scrollSpeed);
        r = new Random();
        this.yGround = yGround;
        barEndUp = new Rectangle();
        barEndDown = new Rectangle();
        barUp = new Rectangle();
        barDown = new Rectangle();
        isScored = false;
```

Author: Create a Pipe class and use the Scrollable class, use the Random() and create new rectangle for texture.

```java
@Override
    public void reset(float newX) {
            super.reset(newX);
            height = r.nextInt(90) + 15;
            isScored = false;
}
```

Pipes need to be reset for next pipe show up.

```java
@Override public void update(float delta) {
        super.update(delta);
        barUp.set(position.x, position.y, width, height);
        barDown.set(position.x, position.y + height + VERTICAL_GAP, width, yGround -
(position.y + height + VERTICAL_GAP));
        barEndUp.set(position.x - (BAR_END_WIDTH - width) / 2, position.y + height -
BAR_END_HEIGHT, BAR_END_WIDTH, BAR_END_HEIGHT);
        barEndDown.set(position.x - (BAR_END_WIDTH - width) / 2, barDown.y,
BAR_END_WIDTH, BAR_END_HEIGHT);
}
```

Author: The Override function will update new pipes and the position.

Flappy Bird using Java

```java
public boolean collides(Bird bird) {
        if (position.x < bird.getX() + bird.getWidth()) {
                return (Intersector.overlaps(bird.getCircle(), barUp) ||
Intersector.overlaps(bird.getCircle(), barDown) ||
                        Intersector.overlaps(bird.getCircle(), barEndUp) ||
Intersector.overlaps(bird.getCircle(), barEndDown));
        }
        return false;
}

        // scroll grass
        if (frontGrass.isScrolledLeft()) {
                frontGrass.reset(backGrass.getTailX());
        }
        else if (backGrass.isScrolledLeft()) {
                backGrass.reset(frontGrass.getTailX());
        }
}
```

Author: In the pipe class, also check the pipe collision using the Intersector.overlaps() vs. The bird. This is called by the ScrollHandler.

Flappy Bird using Java

```java
public Scrollable(float x, float y, int width, int height, float scrollSpeed) {
            position = new Vector2(x, y);
            velocity = new Vector2(scrollSpeed, 0);
            this.width = width;
            this.height = height;
            isScrolledLeft = false;
}
```

Author: In the Scrollable class, this function is null. The position (x, y), width, height, and scrolling speed are from another source. Scrolling function is using the math to set the position and velocity for scrolling. The math is using import com.badlogic.gdx.math.Vector2;

```java
public void update(float delta) {
            position.add(velocity.cpy().scl(delta));
            if (position.x + width < 0) {
                    isScrolledLeft = true;
            }
}
```

Aut
hor: The Scrollable keeps updating.

Flappy Bird using C#

```
region Using Statements
using System;
using System.Collections.Generic;
using System.Linq;
#endregion

namespace FlappyBird
{
#if WINDOWS || LINUX
    /// <summary>
    /// The main class.
    /// </summary>
    public static class Program
    {
        /// <summary>
        /// The main entry point for the application.
        /// </summary>
        [STAThread]
        static void Main()
        {
            using (var game = new FlappyGame())
                game.Run();
        }
    }
#endif
}
```

Author: Start a clean coding including the headers using System; using
System.Collections.Generic; and using System.linq; The entire program will be on the same work
space named FlappyBird. Create a main class Program and in the main function declares an object
to link to FlappyGame class.

Flappy Bird using C#

```
#region Using Statements
using System;
using System.Collections.Generic;
using Microsoft.Xna.Framework;
using Microsoft.Xna.Framework.Content;
using Microsoft.Xna.Framework.Graphics;
using Microsoft.Xna.Framework.Input;
using Microsoft.Xna.Framework.Storage;
using System.Timers;
using System.Diagnostics;
#endregion
```

Author: Frameworks to load the contents and use the clock.

```
  public FlappyGame() : base()
      {
        _graphics = new GraphicsDeviceManager(this);
        Content.RootDirectory = "Content";

        _graphics.PreferredBackBufferHeight = Statics.GAME_HEIGHT;
        _graphics.PreferredBackBufferWidth = Statics.GAME_WIDTH;
        _graphics.SynchronizeWithVerticalRetrace = true;
        _graphics.ApplyChanges();
}
```

Author: In the FlappyGame Class, create a function to use the contents in the folder and set the screen size.

Flappy Bird using C#

```
protected override void Initialize()
    {
        this.Window.Title = Statics.GAME_TITLE;

        Statics.GAME_CONTENT = Content;
        Statics.GAME_GRAPHICSDEVICE = GraphicsDevice;

        Statics.GAME_BACKGROUND = new Layers.Background();
        Statics.GAME_FOREGROUND = new Layers.Foreground();

        Statics.MANAGER_FONT = new Managers.FontManager();
        Statics.MANAGER_INPUT = new Managers.InputManager();
        Statics.MANAGER_SCREEN = new Managers.ScreenManager();
        Statics.MANAGER_SOUND = new Managers.SoundManager();
        Statics.MANAGER_TEXTURES = new Managers.TextureManager();
        Statics.MANAGER_UI = new Managers.UIManager();

        Statics.GAME_CLOCK = _gameClock;
        _gameClock.Elapsed += new ElapsedEventHandler(OnGameClock_Event);
        _gameClock.Enabled = false;

        base.Initialize();
}
```

Author: Using the protect function to access within the class and by derived classs instance. The override accesses the same function in the other class. The function will override the base function. The GraphicDevice, Layers and Managers are defined in a header file. Inside the Initialize(), it starts new Background (), Foreground(), FontManager(), ScreenManager(), SoundManager(), TextureManager(), UIManager() and start the game clock. _gameClock is a global variable declared within the class. Create each class for Background, Foreground, FontManager, ScreenManager, SoundManager, TextureManager, UIManager to include functions like LoadContent(), Update(), and Draw().

```
private void OnGameClock_Event(object source, ElapsedEventArgs e)
    {
        Statics.TIME_ACTUALGAMETIME += _gameClockTick;
}
```

Author: This function counts the clock. The private function is only accessiable within the class. _gameClockTick is a global variable declared in the class.

Flappy Bird using C#

```
protected override void LoadContent()
    {
        // Create a new SpriteBatch, which can be used to draw textures.
        _spriteBatch = new SpriteBatch(GraphicsDevice);
        Statics.GAME_SPRITEBATCH = _spriteBatch;

        Statics.GAME_BACKGROUND.LoadContent();
        Statics.GAME_FOREGROUND.LoadContent();

        Statics.MANAGER_FONT.LoadContent();
        Statics.MANAGER_TEXTURES.LoadContent();
        Statics.MANAGER_SCREEN.LoadContent();
        Statics.MANAGER_SOUND.LoadContent();
        Statics.MANAGER_UI.LoadContent();

        foreach (Screens.Screen screen in Statics.MANAGER_SCREEN.Stack.Values)
        {
            screen.LoadContent();
        }

        Statics.SCREEN_CURRENT = Statics.MANAGER_SCREEN.Stack["Title"];
}
```

Author: Using the loop to load the contents through out the game. SpriteBatch,
GAME_BACKGROUND, GAME_FOREGROUND, MANAGER_FONT,
MANAGER_TEXTURES, MANAGER_SCREEN, MANAGER_SOUND, MANAGER_UI are
defined in a header file. This function reuses the LoadContent() of each.

Flappy Bird using C#

```csharp
protected override void Update(GameTime gameTime)
{
    if (Statics.MANAGER_INPUT.IsKeyPressed(Keys.F12))
        _graphics.ToggleFullScreen();

    // Check the current game state
    switch (Statics.GAME_STATE)
    {
        case Statics.STATE.Exit:
            {
                Statics.GAME_CLOCK.Enabled = false;
                this.Exit();

                break;
            }
        case Statics.STATE.GameOver:
            {
                Statics.GAME_CLOCK.Enabled = false;
                SetBackgroundLayerScrolling(false);

                break;
            }
        case Statics.STATE.Loading:
            {
                Statics.GAME_CLOCK.Enabled = false;
                SetBackgroundLayerScrolling(true);

                break;
            }
        case Statics.STATE.Paused:
            {
                Statics.GAME_CLOCK.Enabled = false;
                SetBackgroundLayerScrolling(false);

                break;
            }
        case Statics.STATE.Playing:
            {
                if (!Statics.GAME_CLOCK.Enabled)
                    Statics.GAME_CLOCK.Enabled = true;

                Statics.GAME_GAMETIME = gameTime;
                SetBackgroundLayerScrolling(true);

                break;
            }
```

```
    }

    Statics.MANAGER_INPUT.Update();
    Statics.MANAGER_UI.Update();
```

Flappy Bird in C#

```
    Statics.SCREEN_CURRENT.Update();

    Statics.MANAGER_SCREEN.Stack["Debug"].Update();

    Statics.GAME_BACKGROUND.Update();
    Statics.GAME_FOREGROUND.Update();

    base.Update(gameTime);
    }
```

Author: The Update() checks game status. If the status is playing, the game clock is true, and SetBackgroundLayerScrolling is true.

Flappy Bird using C#

```csharp
protected override void Draw(GameTime gameTime)
    {
        GraphicsDevice.Clear(Color.DeepSkyBlue);

        Statics.GAME_BACKGROUND.Draw();
        Statics.SCREEN_CURRENT.Draw();
        Statics.GAME_FOREGROUND.Draw();

        Statics.MANAGER_UI.Draw();

        Statics.MANAGER_SCREEN.Stack["Debug"].Draw();

        base.Draw(gameTime);
    }
}
```

Author: To draw the game, the screen is set to blue, and the time is updated.

Flappy Bird using C#

```
private void SetBackgroundLayerScrolling(bool isScrolling)
    {
        foreach (ParallaxBackground layer in
Statics.GAME_BACKGROUND.BackgroundLayer_Stack.Values)
        {
            layer.IsScrolling = isScrolling;
        }

        foreach (ParallaxBackground layer in
Statics.GAME_FOREGROUND.ForegroundLayer_Stack.Values)
        {
            layer.IsScrolling = isScrolling;
        }
    }
```

Author: This function is called by the update () to continue scrolling screen or not.

Flappy Bird using C#

```csharp
class Pipe : Entity
    {

        private float _baseSpeed = 4f;

        public Pipe(Type type, float speedModifier) : base(type)
        {

                this.Texture =
                Statics.GAME_CONTENT.Load<Texture2D>("Textures\\Entity\\flappy_pipe");
                this.Position = new Vector2(Statics.GAME_WIDTH,
                Statics.GAME_RANDOM.Next(Statics.GAME_HEIGHT /4 - this.Texture.Height /2,
                Statics.GAME_HEIGHT / 4 - this.Texture.Height / 4));
                this.Width = this.Texture.Width;
                this.Height = this.Texture.Height;
                this.EntityType = type;
                this.MoveSpeed = _baseSpeed + speedModifier;
                this.ColorData = new Color[this.Width * this.Height];
                this.Texture.GetData(ColorData);

        }

    }
```

Author: Create a class named Pipe, then create a function to add the pipe to the game. Set the object and the speed.

Flappy Bird using C#

```csharp
public override void Update()
    {
        if (Statics.GAME_STATE == Statics.STATE.Playing)
        {
            if (Statics.GAME_USESLOWMODE)
                this.Position.X -= this.MoveSpeed * Statics.GAME_SPEED_DIFFICULTY *
Statics.GAME_SLOWMODERATE;
            else
                this.Position.X -= this.MoveSpeed * Statics.GAME_SPEED_DIFFICULTY;
        }
    }

    public override void Draw()
    {
        Statics.GAME_SPRITEBATCH.Begin();
        Statics.GAME_SPRITEBATCH.Draw(this.Texture, this.Position, Color.White);
        Statics.GAME_SPRITEBATCH.End();

        base.Draw();
    }
}
```

Author In the Pipe class, the two Update() and Draw() will update the postition and draw the texture using the same or preexiting texture for the pipe.

Flappy Bird using C#

```csharp
class Bird : Entity
  {

        private AnimatedSprite _bird_Sprite;
        private float _ySpeed;
        public bool UseSlowFall = false;
        public bool UseJumpBoost = false;
        public bool UseStarPower = false;

  public Bird(Type type) : base(type)
      {
        this.Texture = Statics.MANAGER_TEXTURES.Textures["Entity\\DeadBird"];
        this.Position = new Vector2(300, 300);
        this.Rotation = 0f;
        this.Scale = .75f;
        this.EntityType = type;
        this.Width = this.Texture.Width;
        this.Height = this.Texture.Height;
        this.MoveSpeed = 5f;
        this.ColorData = new Color[this.Width * this.Height];
        this.Texture.GetData(ColorData);

        Texture2D texture = Statics.MANAGER_TEXTURES.AnimatedTextures["Entity\\Bird"];

        _bird_Sprite = new AnimatedSprite();
        _bird_Sprite.Initialize(texture, this.Position, this.Rotation, 128, 128, 4, 60, Color.White,
this.Scale, true);

        _ySpeed = 0f;
      }
```

Author: Create a class called Bird Create, set the position, and the moving speed.

Flappy Bird using C#

```csharp
public override void Update()
{
    if (Statics.GAME_STATE == Statics.STATE.Playing)
    {
        _ySpeed += UseSlowFall ? .5f : .75f;

        CheckForInput();

        this.Position.Y = MathHelper.Clamp(this.Position.Y, (this.Height * this.Scale),
Statics.GAME_FLOOR + this.Height * _bird_Sprite.Scale);

        if (this.Position.Y < Statics.GAME_FLOOR)
        {
            this.Position.Y += _ySpeed;
        }
        else
        {
            Statics.GAME_STATE = Statics.STATE.GameOver;
        }

        this.Rotation = (float)Math.Atan2(_ySpeed, 10);

        _bird_Sprite.Position = this.Position;
        _bird_Sprite.Rotation = this.Rotation;
        _bird_Sprite.Update(Statics.GAME_GAMETIME);
    }
}
```

Author: In the bird class, this function checks the game status and user input. It uses the MathHelper and the Math to clamp the bird position.

Flappy Bird using C#

```csharp
public override void Draw()

    {

        if (Statics.GAME_STATE == Statics.STATE.GameOver)

        {

            Statics.GAME_SPRITEBATCH.Begin();

            Statics.GAME_SPRITEBATCH.Draw(this.Texture, _bird_Sprite.Bounds, new
Rectangle(0, 0, _bird_Sprite.FrameWidth, _bird_Sprite.FrameHeight), Color.White,
_bird_Sprite.Rotation, _bird_Sprite.SourceRotate, SpriteEffects.None, 1.0f);

            Statics.GAME_SPRITEBATCH.End();

        }

        else

        {

            _bird_Sprite.Draw(Statics.GAME_SPRITEBATCH);

        }


        base.Draw();

    }
```

Author: This is the draw function. If the game state is over, it will draw a new bird. It is actually created a texture with zero size. The bird itself is an image file.

Flappy Bird using C#

```
private void CheckForInput()
    {
        if (Statics.MANAGER_INPUT.IsKeyPressed(Keys.Space) ||
Statics.MANAGER_INPUT.IsLeftMouseClicked())
            Jump();

        if (Statics.MANAGER_INPUT.CurrentGamePadState().DPad.Up == ButtonState.Pressed)
            Jump();

        if (Statics.MANAGER_INPUT.IsGamepadPressed(Buttons.A))
            Jump();

        if (Statics.MANAGER_INPUT.IsKeyPressed(Keys.D1))
            UseJumpBoost = UseJumpBoost ? false : true;

        if (Statics.MANAGER_INPUT.IsKeyPressed(Keys.D2))
            UseSlowFall = UseSlowFall ? false : true;

        // Input : Gamepad
        this.Position.X +=
Statics.MANAGER_INPUT.CurrentGamePadState().ThumbSticks.Left.X * this.MoveSpeed;
    }
```

Author: Check User input to move the bird.

Flappy Bird using C#

```
private void Jump()
    {
        Statics.MANAGER_SOUND.Play("Player\\Jump");

        _ySpeed = UseJumpBoost ? -14 : -8;
}
```

Author: Jump with sound

Flappy Bird using C#

```csharp
namespace FlappyBird.Helpers
{
  class Collision
  {
    public static bool IsSloppyCollision(Rectangle sprite1Rectangle, Rectangle sprite2Rectangle)
    {
      return sprite1Rectangle.Intersects(sprite2Rectangle);
    }

    public static bool IsPixelCollision(Rectangle sprite1Rectangle, Rectangle sprite2Rectangle,
Color[] colorData1, Color[] colorData2)
    {
      bool hasCollided = false;

      if (sprite1Rectangle.Intersects(sprite2Rectangle))
      {
        int _top = Math.Max(sprite1Rectangle.Top, sprite2Rectangle.Top);
        int _bottom = Math.Min(sprite1Rectangle.Bottom, sprite2Rectangle.Bottom);
        int _left = Math.Max(sprite1Rectangle.Left, sprite2Rectangle.Left);
        int _right = Math.Min(sprite1Rectangle.Right, sprite2Rectangle.Right);

        try
        {
          for (int yA = _top; yA < _bottom; yA++)
          {
            // For each pixel in this row
            for (int xA = _left; xA < _right; xA++)
            {

              Color colorA = colorData1[(xA - sprite1Rectangle.Left) + (yA -
sprite1Rectangle.Top) * sprite1Rectangle.Width];
              Color colorB = colorData2[(xA - sprite2Rectangle.Left) + (yA -
sprite2Rectangle.Top) * sprite2Rectangle.Width];

              // If both pixels are not completely transparent,
              if (colorA.A > 0 && colorB.A > 0)
              {
                // then an intersection has been found
                hasCollided = true;
              }
            }
          }
        }
        catch (Exception ex)
        {
          System.Diagnostics.Debug.WriteLine("Exception occured while checking for pixel
```

```
collision. " + ex.InnerException);
            }
        }

        return hasCollided;
    }
  }
}
```

Author: The collided class has a collided function which uses the bool type to return true or false. If the bird hits the object by finding the pixels and points of transparent intersection, the collision returns true. This is the main action of this game. The rest is just loading the contents.

Flappy Bird using HTML5 and JavaScript

```
<!DOCTYPE html>
<html>
  <head>
    <meta charset="utf-8">
    <title>Canvas Bird</title>
    <link rel="stylesheet" href="index.css">
  </head>
  <body>
    <canvas id="canvas" width="640" height="480"></canvas>

    <script src="app.js"></script>
  </body>
</html>
```

Author: Create a basic html to use index.css and app.js

Flappy Bird using HTML5 and JavaScript

```css
@import url(https://fonts.googleapis.com/css?family=Raleway);

*, html, body {
   box-sizing: border-box;
   font-family: 'Raleway', Arial;
}

#canvas {
   border: 1px solid;
}
```

Author: In the index.css, link to Google online font and set the screen border line to 1px solid.

Flappy Bird using HTML5 and JavaScript

```
(function() {
    //Get canvas and context
    var c   = document.getElementById('canvas'),
ctx = c.getContext('2d');
```

Author: Start writing app.js to include canvas and context

```
 //Load assets
    var bgImg = loadImage('assets/background.jpg', 640, 480),
        playerImg = loadImage('assets/player.png', 192, 64),
        enemyUpImg = loadImage('assets/enemy_up.png', 64, 316),
        enemyDownImg = loadImage('assets/enemy_down.png', 64, 316);

    var pointAudio = new Audio('assets/point.mp3'),
        loseAudio = new Audio('assets/lose.mp3');

    //Helper methods
    function loadImage(src, width, height) {
        var img = new Image(width, height);
        img.src = src;
return img;
```

Author: Loading the assets by declaring each object to LoadImage(ImageLocation, width, height) and Audio(mp3 file location)

Flappy Bird using HTML5 and JavaScript

```
//Register event handlers & kick off the game
  window.onload = function() {
    c.addEventListener('click', function() {
      if (PLAYER_CONTROLS_ON) {
        player.jump();
      }
      if (!GAME_PLAYING) {
        resetGame();
        GAME_PLAYING = true;
        PLAYER_CONTROLS_ON = true;
      }
    });

    update();
};
```

Author: This is the main function. It calls jump(), resetGame() and update(). The jump function returns a negative velocity first which the bird will fall down unless the player press the key.

```
  function resetGame() {
    scoreCounter.reset();
    player.reset();
    setupEnemies();
}
```

Author: Inside the resetGame(), it calls setupEnemies() to draw the pipes.

Flappy Bird using HTML5 and JavaScript

```
//Set up initial enemy positions before rendering them
  var enemies = [];
  function setupEnemies() {
    nextEnemyId = 0;
    lastEnemyId = ENEMY_NUMBER - 1; //used to reposition enemies

    for (var i = 0; i < ENEMY_NUMBER; i++) {
      var yOffset = randomIntFromInterval(MIN_YOFFSET, MAX_YOFFSET);
      var enemySet = {
        enemyUp: new Enemy(i, c.height / 2, yOffset),
        enemyDown: new Enemy(i, 0, yOffset, false)
      };
      enemies[i] = enemySet;
    }
  }
```

Author: The setupEnemies() and Enemy() randomly create the top pipe and bottom pipe using ramdonIntFromInterval.

Flappy Bird using HTML5 and JavaScript

```
function Enemy(id, y, yOffset, imgDirectionIsUp, speed, img) {
    if (typeof id === 'undefined') throw new Error('Parameter ID must be defined');
    this.id = id;
    this.imgDirectionIsUp = typeof imgDirectionIsUp === 'undefined' ? true : imgDirectionIsUp;
    this.yOffset = yOffset || 0;

    this.x = c.width + id * ENEMY_OFFSET || 0;
    if
        (this.imgDirectionIsUp) this.y = y + ENEMY_DISTANCE + this.yOffset || 0;
    else
        this.y = y - ENEMY_DISTANCE + this.yOffset || 0;

    this.speed = speed || 3;
    this.img = img || (this.imgDirectionIsUp ? enemyUpImg : enemyDownImg);
}
```

Author: Create the pipes obove and below with the speed.

Flappy Bird using HTML5 and JavaScript

```
//******* Player Object **********//
   //fps locking vars
   var fpsCounter = Date.now(), //custom timer to restrict fps
      fps = 30;
   //free falling counter
   var fallingCounter = Date.now();
   //Player
      player = {
      //private state
      _currentFrame: 0,

      //public properties
      //physics
      velocity: 2,
      force: 0.15,
      //positional
      x: 70,
      y: 20,
      width: 64,
      height: 64,

      //methods
      jump: function() {
         this.velocity = -6;
      },
      fall: function() {
         var now = Date.now();
         if (now - fallingCounter > 1000 / fps) {
            if (this.velocity < 8) this.velocity += this.force;
            this.y += this.velocity;
         }
      }
},
```

Author: Create a player class, In the class, create a jump() returns velocity -6, but set the default velocity to 2. Start with negative velocity and increment.

Flappy Bird using HTML5 and JavaScript

```javascript
//Main functions
  var updateLoop;
  function update() {
    draw();
    updateLoop = window.requestAnimationFrame(update);
  }

  function draw() {
    //Set font style
    ctx.font = '48px Raleway';
    //Clean canvas
    ctx.clearRect(0, 0, c.width, c.height);
    //Draw next frame with props
    drawBackground();
    //If game hasn't started or player lost show splash screen text
    if (!GAME_PLAYING) {
      ctx.strokeStyle = 'rgba(0,0,0,' + textAlpha.get() + ')';
      ctx.strokeText('Click to start game', c.width / 2 - 230, 80);
      ctx.fillStyle = 'rgba(255,255,255,' + textAlpha.get() + ')';
      ctx.fillText('Click to start game', c.width / 2 - 230, 80);
      textAlpha.fluctuate();
    }
    //If game is playing draw everything
    else {
      drawEnemies();
      drawPlayer();
      //Draw the score
      ctx.fillStyle = 'black';
      ctx.strokeText(scoreCounter.getScore(), c.width / 2 - 11, 51);
      ctx.fillStyle = 'white';
      ctx.fillText(scoreCounter.getScore(), c.width / 2 - 10, 50);
    }
  }
}
```

Author: The update() calls draw() to call drawBackground(), drawEnemies(), DrawPlayer() and getScore().

Flappy Bird using HTML5 and JavaScript

```javascript
//Instantiate, draw and animate backgrounds
  var bg1 = new Background(0, 0);
  var bg2 = new Background(c.width, 0);

  function drawBackground() {
    ctx.drawImage(bg1.img, bg1.x, bg1.y);
    ctx.drawImage(bg2.img, bg2.x, bg2.y);
    bg1.move();
    bg2.move();
}
```

Author: Sart new background, call drawImage() and move().

```javascript
//******* Background Constructor **********//
  function Background(x, y, speed, img) {
    this.x = x || 0;
    this.y = y || 0;
    this.img  = img || bgImg;
    this.speed = speed || 1;
  }
  Background.prototype = {
    move: function() {
      this.x -= this.speed;
      if (this.x <= -this.img.width) {
        this.x = c.width;
      }
    }
  };
```

Author: The Background class move() to move the object backward using the width.

Flappy Bird using HTML5 and JavaScript

```
function drawEnemies() {
    for (var i = 0; i < enemies.length; i++) {
        ctx.drawImage(enemies[i].enemyUp.img, enemies[i].enemyUp.x, enemies[i].enemyUp.y);
        ctx.drawImage(enemies[i].enemyDown.img, enemies[i].enemyDown.x,
enemies[i].enemyDown.y);
        enemies[i].enemyUp.move();
        enemies[i].enemyDown.move();
    }
}
```

Author: Using the loop to continue to create the block objects on top and at the bottom. Call the move() to move the object too.

```
Enemy.prototype = {
    move: function() {
        this.x -= this.speed;
        if (this.x <= -this.img.width && this.imgDirectionIsUp) {
            //Set x of this enemy set to next enemy set + enemy offset
            this.x = enemies[this.id].enemyDown.x = enemies[lastEnemyId].enemyUp.x +
ENEMY_OFFSET;
            //Set new random Y
            this.yOffset = enemies[this.id].enemyDown.yOffset =
randomIntFromInterval(MIN_YOFFSET, MAX_YOFFSET);
            //Update last enemy ID
            lastEnemyId = lastEnemyId === ENEMY_NUMBER - 1 ? 0 : lastEnemyId + 1;
        }
        if (this.id === nextEnemyId && this.x + this.img.width < player.x + player.width) {
            //Update next enemy ID
            nextEnemyId = nextEnemyId === ENEMY_NUMBER - 1 ? 0 : nextEnemyId + 1;
            //Increase the score
            if (PLAYER_CONTROLS_ON) scoreCounter.increaseScore();
        }
    }
};
```

Author: The move() in Enemy class also uses randomIntFromInterval to move the pipes same as the setupEnemy().

Flappy Bird using HTML5 and JavaScript

```
function drawPlayer() {
    //render player
    ctx.drawImage(playerImg, player.getNextFrame() * player.width, 0, //crop start
            player.width, player.height, //crop end
            player.x, player.y, //player pos
            player.width, player.height); //player sprite size
    //move player
    player.fall();
    //collision check
    if (player.hasCollided()) {
        //deactivate player controls
        PLAYER_CONTROLS_ON = false;
        //when player falls of screen stop game
        if (player.y - player.height > c.height) GAME_PLAYING = false;
    }
}
```

Author: It creates the bird. By default, the bird falls itself. The hasCollided() check for collission.

Flappy Bird using HTML5 and JavaScript

```javascript
hasCollided: function() {
    var hasCollided = false;

    var playerX  = this.x + this.width,
        playerTopY    = this.y,
        playerBottomY = this.y + this.height;

    var enemyX = enemies[nextEnemyId].enemyDown.x + 40,
        enemyLookingDownY = enemies[nextEnemyId].enemyDown.y +
enemies[nextEnemyId].enemyDown.img.height,
        enemyLookingUpY = enemies[nextEnemyId].enemyUp.y,
        enemyWidth = enemies[nextEnemyId].enemyDown.img.width;

    //when the enemy is inside an obstacle
    if (playerX > enemyX && playerX < enemyX + enemyWidth - 40) {
        //check for collision and tag player as collided if they hit an obstacle
        if (playerTopY < enemyLookingDownY || playerBottomY > enemyLookingUpY)
            hasCollided = true;
    }

    //if the player goes above/below screen tag as collided
    if (playerBottomY < 0 || playerTopY > c.height) {
        hasCollided = true;
    }

    if (hasCollided & PLAYER_CONTROLS_ON) loseAudio.play();

    //return collision result
    return hasCollided;
},
reset: function() {
    this.velocity = 2;
    this.y = 20;
},
getNextFrame: function() {
    var now = Date.now();
    if (now - fpsCounter > 1000 / fps) {
        fpsCounter = now;
        this._currentFrame++;
        if (this._currentFrame > 2) this._currentFrame = 0;
    }
    return this._currentFrame;
}
};
```

Author: Return true if the bird is inside the object points by pixel width and height. Return true if the bird is above the object hight or below the the object.

Flappy Bird using HTML5 and JavaScript

```javascript
var scoreCounter = {
    //state
    _score: 0,
    //methods
    increaseScore: function() {
        this._score++;
        pointAudio.play();
    },
    getScore: function() {
        return this._score;
    },
    reset: function() {
        this._score = 0;
    }
};
```

Author: In the class, create a score function, set default score to zero and count++, call pointAudio() object to play audio. Create a function to return score, and a reset functio to reset score for easy to use in coding.

Multiplayer Online Game Server

```
/*
  MIT Licensed. See LICENSE for full license.
  Usage : node simplest.app.js
*/
  var
     gameport        = process.env.PORT || 4004,
     io              = require('socket.io'),
     express         = require('express'),
     UUID            = require('node-uuid'),
     verbose         = false,
     app             = express.createServer();
```

```
/* Express server set up. */
//The express server handles passing our content to the browser,
//As well as routing users where they need to go. This example is bare bones
//and will serve any file the user requests from the root of your web server (where you launch the
script from)
//so keep this in mind - this is not a production script but a development teaching tool.
```

```
    //Tell the server to listen for incoming connections
  app.listen( gameport );

    //Log something so we know that it succeeded.
  console.log('\t :: Express :: Listening on port ' + gameport );

    //By default, we forward the / path to index.html automatically.
  app.get( '/', function( req, res ){
     res.sendfile( __dirname + '/simplest.html' );
  });

    //This handler will listen for requests on /*, any file from the root of our server.
    //See expressjs documentation for more info on routing.

  app.get( '/*' , function( req, res, next ) {

       //This is the current file they have requested
     var file = req.params[0];

       //For debugging, we can track what files are requested.
     if(verbose) console.log('\t :: Express :: file requested : ' + file);

       //Send the requesting client the file.
     res.sendfile( __dirname + '/' + file );

  }); //app.get *
```

Author: Create a default HTML index webpage to start the game. It will open a connection port using socket.js. Normally, a Web Browser enables JavaScript RunTime Node.js to run JavaScript. This code requires Socket.io. MIT License is an open source.

Multiplayer Online Game Server

```html
<!DOCTYPE html>
<html>
    <head>
        <title> Real time multi-player games with HTML5</title>
        <style type="text/css">
            html , body {
                background: #212121;
                color: #fff;
                margin: 0;
                padding: 0;
            }
            #canvas {
                position: absolute;
                left: 0; right: 0; top: 0; bottom: 0;
                margin: auto;
            }
        </style>

        <!-- Notice the URL, this is handled by socket.io on the server automatically, via express -->
        <script type="text/javascript" src="/socket.io/socket.io.js"></script>

        <!-- This will create a connection to socket.io, and print the user serverid that we sent from the server side. -->
        <script type="text/javascript">

            //This is all that needs
            var socket = io.connect('/');

            //Now we can listen for that event
            socket.on('onconnected', function( data ) {

                //Note that the data is the object we sent from the server, as is. So we can assume its id exists.
                console.log( 'Connected successfully to the socket.io server. My server side ID is ' + data.id );

            });

        </script>

    </head>
    <body>
        <canvas id="canvas"> </canvas>
    </body>
</html>
```

Author: This is HTML5 Client to Server. The game server may require the user to load or download a simple code or software to connect to the server.